Cookbook

Make your food fun!

Welcome to Planet Cook!

Have a balanced diet!

Cookbook

Recipes by Kevin Woodford

Food photography by
Howard Shooter

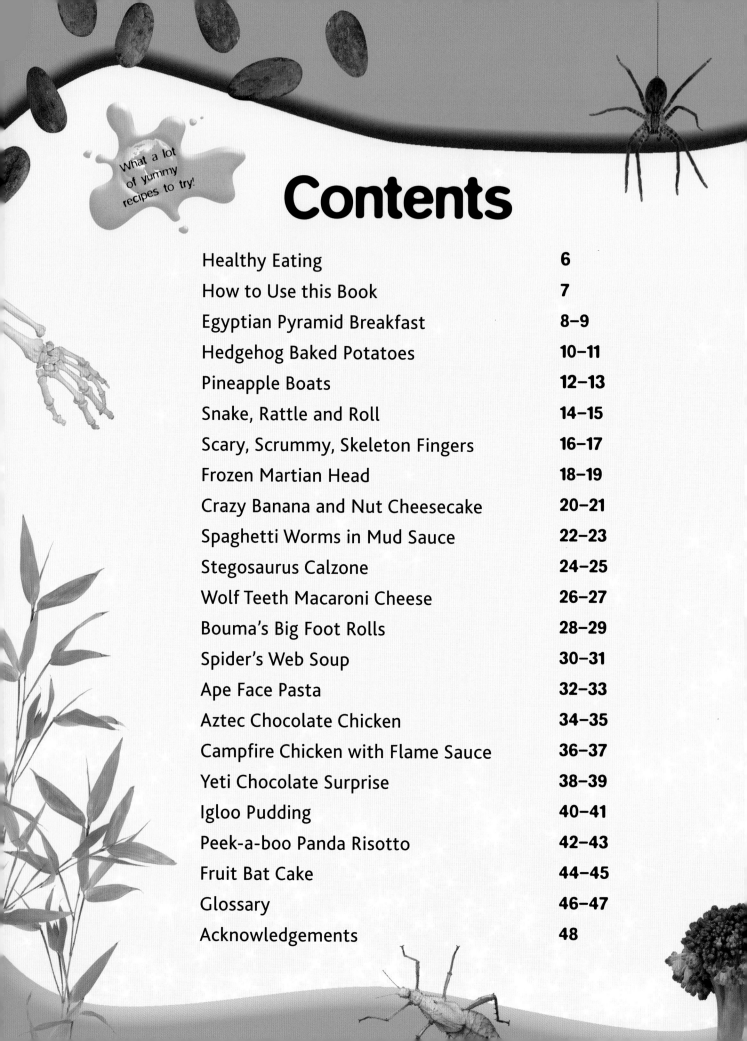

What a lot of yummy recipes to try!

Contents

Planet Cook

Take a celebrity chef, add a spoonful of magic, a sprinkling of fun facts, bring to the boil and you've got a totally unique creative cooking adventure for kids.

Set on a fantasy island, each adventure sees Kevin Woodford (alias Captain Cook) guide three young Cook Cadets and Bouma, a magical yeti, as they create a recipe inspired by the natural world.

A few words from Kevin Woodford:

For over 20 years I have held the belief that the earlier our kids get into the kitchen, the better it will be for them as they grow into adults. I firmly believe that the kitchen is the heart of any home, a place where the family should gather in order to enjoy the experience of creating the family meal.

So I hope that you and your family have as much fun cooking the recipes as we have had creating them.

Captain Cook

Healthy Eating

What you choose to eat is very important. The right food helps keep you fit, healthy and happy. Eating the right food is also known as having a balanced diet. A balanced diet should contain the following types of food:

Carbohydrates

Carbohydrates give you energy so that you can be active and strong all day long. Without them you wouldn't be able to concentrate at school or play sport.

I need energy!

Protein

Protein builds up your muscles and your strength. It helps your body to grow and makes sure that it works properly. You should try to eat some protein in two out of your three meals every day.

Fibre

Fibre is not a nutrient because it is not absorbed by your body, but you need it to keep your bowels healthy. It helps your body digest food and keeps your intestines healthy.

Fat

Fat gives your body energy and allows you to absorb other important nutrients. It also keeps you warm and is a protective cushion for your internal organs. Too much fat is bad for you, so you should always eat sensibly.

Vitamins and Minerals

Vitamins and minerals help your body to grow and repair itself. For example, calcium gives you strong teeth and bones and vitamin C helps your body heal.

I have strong bones!

How to Use this Book

The recipes in this book are specially designed to be easy-to-use and packed full of fun. Follow the step-by-step words and pictures to create some tasty dishes. Read the Info-Bite in the top right corner to find out what has inspired the recipe and then go to www.planetcook.com and discover more, using the password provided.

Read the Info-Bite and use the internet to find out more.

Take extra care and ask an adult for help when you see this symbol.

Assemble the ingredients and tools before you begin cooking.

The pictures will help you understand what to do.

Carefully read the step-by-step text.

Egyptian Pyramid Breakfast

This breakfast recipe might just be the missing eighth wonder of the world! Build your own toast pyramid, just like the real ones in Ancient Egypt. And instead of surrounding it with golden desert sand, try light and fluffy scrambled eggs. What an exciting and different way to serve scrambled eggs on toast!

The Egyptian pyramids are guarded by a statue called the Sphinx.

Ingredients:
- 6 eggs
- 1 tbsp milk
- black pepper
- knob of butter
- 6 slices wholemeal bread
- margarine (optional)

Tools:
- mixing bowl
- fork or whisk
- saucepan or small frying pan
- wooden spoon
- toaster or grill
- bread knife

What a great start to the day!

serves 4

Get cracking!

1. One at a time, tap the eggs on the side of the bowl and pull the shells apart. The insides will drop into the bowl. Add the milk and black pepper to the bowl.

2. Using a fork or whisk, beat the eggs and milk until they are completely blended together. The resulting mixture will be smooth and yellow.

3. Toast the bread, using a toaster or grill and spread a thin layer of margarine on each slice. Carefully, cut the toast in half diagonally to make 12 triangles.

8

Visit: www.planetcook.com   Password: SAND

Eggs contain protein!

Info-Bite
The Ancient Egyptians lived four thousand years ago in Egypt, North Africa. They were ruled by kings called pharaohs. When pharaohs died, they were buried in stone pyramid-shaped tombs. They were buried with their gold and precious objects because they wanted to be wealthy in the afterlife!

4. Put the butter into the saucepan and melt it over a low heat. When it has melted, tilt the pan so that the butter completely covers the base of the pan.

Try adding spring onion palm trees in step 6.

5. Pour the egg mixture into the saucepan and stir with a wooden spoon. As the egg at the bottom of the pan begins to cook, keep stirring to make sure that all the egg cooks.

6. To serve, stand three pieces of toast on a plate to form the pyramid shape. Spoon a serving of scrambled egg around the pyramid.

Top tip: Cut the crusts off the toast if the pyramid won't stand up.

Try adding cooked bacon and tomato in step 5.

9

Check out these splats for extra recipe hints and suggestions.

Basic Cooking Rules

1. Always wash your hands before and after cooking.
2. Read the recipe through before you begin.
3. Be careful, especially when you are using sharp knives or hot things such as the cooker or oven.
4. Ask an adult for help if you need it.
5. Just relax and have a go – cooking should be fun!

Be safe!

Egyptian Pyramid Breakfast

The Egyptian pyramids are guarded by a statue called the Sphinx.

This breakfast recipe might just be the missing eighth wonder of the world! Build your own toast pyramid, just like the real ones in Ancient Egypt. And instead of surrounding it with golden desert sand, try light and fluffy scrambled eggs. What an exciting and different way to serve scrambled eggs on toast!

Ingredients:

- 6 eggs
- 1 tbsp milk
- black pepper
- knob of butter
- 6 slices wholemeal bread
- margarine (optional)

Tools:

- mixing bowl
- fork or whisk
- saucepan or small frying pan
- wooden spoon
- toaster or grill
- bread knife

What a great start to the day!

serves 4

Get cracking!

1. One at a time, tap the eggs on the side of the bowl and pull the shells apart. The insides will drop into the bowl. Add the milk and black pepper to the bowl.

2. Using a fork or whisk, beat the eggs and milk until they are completely blended together. The resulting mixture will be smooth and yellow.

3. Toast the bread, using a toaster or grill and spread a thin layer of margarine on each slice. Carefully, cut the toast in half diagonally to make 12 triangles.

Eggs contain protein!

4. Put the butter into the saucepan and melt it over a low heat. When it has melted, tilt the pan so that the butter completely covers the base of the pan.

Try adding spring onion palm trees in step 6.

5. Pour the egg mixture into the saucepan and stir with a wooden spoon. As the egg at the bottom of the pan begins to cook, keep stirring to make sure that all the egg cooks.

6. To serve, stand three pieces of toast on a plate to form the pyramid shape. Spoon a serving of scrambled egg around the pyramid.

Top tip: cut the crusts off the toast if the pyramid won't stand up.

Try adding cooked bacon and tomato in step 5.

9

Hedgehog Baked Potatoes

Real hedgehogs aren't tasty at all – they roll up into a ball with their prickly spines sticking out so that predators can't eat them. However, these hedgehog baked potatoes taste fantastic, especially the pumpkin seed spines. Experiment with different fillings such as cottage cheese and pineapple, broccoli and cheddar or coleslaw.

You might be lucky enough to see a hedgehog in your garden at night!

Ingredients:

- 2 large baking potatoes (scrubbed clean)
- 200g (7oz) can tuna
- 50g (2oz) sweetcorn
- 50g (2oz) can or jar roasted peppers (diced)
- 1 tbsp of chopped parsley
- 50g (2oz) low-fat cream cheese
- pumpkin seeds
- 1 bag of pre-washed mixed salad leaves
- 2 tbsp extra virgin olive oil
- juice of ½ lemon
- freshly ground black pepper

Tools:

- fork
- sharp knife
- tin opener
- spoon
- 2 bowls
- potato masher

serves 4

Mix it up!

1. Preheat the oven to 200°C (400°F/Gas Mark 6). Prick the skins of the potatoes with a fork and bake them for 1 hour, or until cooked. Leave them to cool.

2. Put the tuna into a bowl. Set aside 4 pieces of pepper and 8 sweetcorn kernels. Mix the rest of the sweetcorn, diced peppers and parsley with the tuna.

3. Using a sharp knife, cut the cooled potatoes in half lengthways. Carefully scoop out the potato flesh using a spoon. Try not to pierce the skin when you do this.

4. Put the potato into a bowl and mash it until smooth. Mix in the low fat cream cheese and season. Add the tuna mixture and then mix it all together.

Hunt these out!

Info-Bite

Nocturnal animals are more active at night than during the day. Most sleep during the day and come out at night to hunt. Hedgehogs, bats, owls, foxes and badgers are all nocturnal. Most mice are also nocturnal and they are hunted by owls who use their amazing eyesight to see their prey in the dark.

5. Spoon the mixture back into the potato skins to form the hedgehogs. Stick the pumpkin seeds into the mound of potato to make the hedgehogs' spines.

6. Choose which end is the front of the hedgehog and make the face – stick in a piece of pepper for the nose and add 2 pieces of sweetcorn for the eyes.

7. Put the potatoes back into the oven and bake them for 15 minutes, or until they are heated through. Leave them to cool for a couple of minutes before eating them.

Serve your hedgehog baked potatoes with a green salad.

Pineapple Boats

Sail away on your own taste-sensation creation!

Everyone knows that fresh fruit is good for you, but don't you sometimes wish that it could be more interesting? After all, most of the time you just have to wash it, maybe peel it and then eat it and where's the fun in that? Well, with this imaginative recipe fresh fruit can stimulate your imagination as well as your taste buds!

Ingredients:

- 1 large pineapple
- 1 medium orange
- glacé cherries or grapes
- 4 cocktail sticks or drinking straws (cut to size)

serves 4

Tools:

- sharp knife
- chopping board
- cocktail sticks

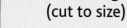

Fresh fruit is tasty and good for you!

1. Ask an adult to cut the pineapple in half lengthways, leaving the leafy tops intact. They should cut each piece in half again, also lengthways. You should now have 4 quarters of pineapple.

2. Remove the core from the centre of the pineapple quarters. Then carefully slide the knife to detach the flesh from the skin. Without removing the flesh from the shell, chop it into 1cm (½ in) cubes.

3. To make the boats' sails, cut four thin slices from the orange. Carefully insert a cocktail stick through the bottom of each slice of orange.

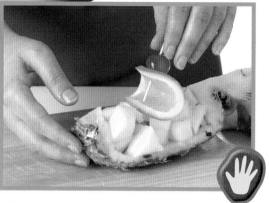

4. Place a glacé cherry or grape on the top of each cocktail stick. Then carefully push the stick through the top of the orange slice and gently push the sail into the boat.

Info-Bite

Lots of animals are so tiny that you can only see them through a microscope or magnifying glass. For example, did you know that tiny fleas live in the fur of cats and dogs and feed on their blood? However, not all tiny living things are bad news – friendly bacteria found in food like yoghurt can help you to digest food.

5. Place a pineapple boat onto each plate. They taste delicious like this or you could try serving them with a dollop of ice cream or frozen yoghurt.

If you don't like glacé cherries, use fresh cherries or grapes instead.

Fresh fruit tastes great!

You should eat fruit everyday.

Snake, Rattle and Roll

A love of snakes is called ophiophilia; a fear of snakes is called ophidiophobia.

With their forked tongues and beady eyes, snakes can look pretty sssscary and many species could kill you with a single bite! Rattlesnakes have a rattle on the end of their tails which they use as a warning when they feel threatened. Sink your fangs into this rattlesnake-inspired sausage roll, before it slithers away. Delicioussssssssss!

Ingredients:
- 225g (8oz) puff pastry
- 225g (8oz) sausage meat
- handful of flour
- 1 egg (beaten)
- sesame seeds
- sunflower seeds
- poppy seeds
- paprika (optional)
- foil (for a forked tongue and rattle)

Tools:
- baking tray
- rolling pin
- pastry brush

What a ssssuper sausage roll!

serves 8

Let's roll it!

1. Preheat the oven to 210°C (425°F/Gas Mark 7). Divide the puff pastry in half, lengthways. Roll out each piece into a rectangle, about 2–3 mm thick.

2. Join the two pastry sheets together at a shorter end, to make a longer piece. Brush the pastry with a little beaten egg and press down firmly. Sprinkle with paprika.

3. Mould the sausage meat into a long, thin shape and place it in the middle of the pastry sheet. Brush the edges of the pastry with some more beaten egg.

Hissssssss

4. Wrap the pastry around the sausage to make a long sausage roll. Seal the edges together and turn it over so that this edge is underneath. Grease a baking tray.

Info-Bite

Snakes are cold-blooded animals so they need the sun to keep warm. They have no legs but they can slither very fast on their bellies. Snakes are carnivores and use their forked tongues to smell. Their scaly skin doesn't stretch like ours so as they get bigger they shed their old skins to reveal new skin underneath.

5. Place the roll onto the baking tray. Bend it to form a snake shape. Brush it with beaten egg and add some poppy and sesame seeds to make a snake pattern.

6. Cut a tail and forked tongue from foil. Add some sesame seeds to the tail and fix it to the snake. Fix the tongue to the other end and add sunflower seed eyes.

7. Bake the sausage roll in the oven for 20 minutes, or until golden. Allow it to cool on the baking tray. When it is cool, sprinkle on lots more sunflower seeds.

Vegetarians could use a filling of cheese and cooked potato instead of sausage meat.

Serve the sausage roll with a green salad such as cress or rocket.

Scary, Scrummy, Skeleton Fingers

hy didn't the skeleton go to the ball?
ecause he had no body to go with!

Skeletons don't have to be spooky – in fact, with a little bit of imagination they can be a delicious meal! This recipe gives your favourite fish fingers a scary, scrummy Planet Cook makeover. Follow the simple steps below and make not just the fingers, but a whole skeleton hand! Serve with a dollop of gory finger sauce. Spooooky!

Ingredients:

Bony fingers:
• 4 fillets of sole or plaice (skinned)
• 50g (2oz) plain flour
• pepper
• 2 eggs (beaten)
• 100g (4oz) dried breadcrumbs

Palm of the hand (Bubble and Squeak):
• 1 tbsp olive oil
• 450g (16oz) mashed potato
• 100g (4oz) cooked cabbage

• 100g (4oz) cooked carrot (mashed)
• pinch of grated nutmeg
• freshly ground black pepper
• 1–2 tbsp olive oil

For finger sauce:
• 4 tbsp low fat mayonnaise
• 1 tbsp snipped chives
• 1 tsp Worcestershire sauce
• 2 tbsp tomato ketchup

Tools:

• sharp knife
• chopping board
• baking sheet
• mixing bowl
• wooden spoon
• frying pan
• small dish for the finger sauce

serve
4

spoooooky!

1. Preheat the oven to 190°C (375°F/Gas Mark 5). Cut each piece of fish into five fingers. Roll them in the flour and shake off any extra. Dip them into the egg and breadcrumbs.

2. Roll them on a clean board to remove any excess breadcrumbs. Chill them for 10 minutes. Put them on an oiled baking tray and cook for 15–20 minutes, turning once.

3. To make the palm of the hand, mix the mashed potato, cabbage and mashed carrots together in a bowl. Season with a little grated nutmeg and pepper.

4. Heat the oil in a frying pan and add the potato mixture. Stir constantly over a medium heat for 6 to 8 minutes. The potato will turn golden and crispy.

Info-Bite

There are more than 200 bones in the human skeleton. They protect important parts inside your body such as your brain and your heart. Your bones grow as you do and have muscles attached which help your body to move. Calcium makes your bones strong and that's why it's important to drink lots of milk.

5. Mix all the finger sauce ingredients together and serve in a small dish. Place a portion of the potato mixture onto a plate and shape it into the palm of a hand. Add four fingers and a thumb.

Always pay attention when stirring hot food!

If you don't have time to make the sauce, ketchup is fine.

The cabbage and carrot contain fibre, vitamins and minerals.

Frozen Martian Head

Here is another idea of what a martian could look like!

Take your taste buds to another planet with this fruity frozen dessert! No one really knows what's out there, but one thing's for sure – this yummy dessert is out of this world! Let your imagination run riot and use interesting sweets to create your martian's face. Who says that martians would have two eyes or just one nose? Go for it!

Ingredients:
- 500ml (20fl oz) tub strawberry ice cream
- 4 large strawberries
- 125g (4oz) raspberries
- 1 tbsp honey
- 1 small banana
- 1 small packet of liquorice allsorts
- 2 small plums or large grapes
- 2 plain biscuits

Tools:
- 600ml (1 pint) glass bowl
- clingfilm
- spoon
- sharp knife
- potato masher or fork

Read the recipe first!

serves 4

Let's ffffreeze it!

1. Line the bowl with clingfilm. Use 3 quarters of the ice cream to cover the sides and base of the bowl but leave a well in the centre. Freeze for 30 minutes.

2. Remove the green stalks from the strawberries and cut the strawberries and raspberries into quarters. Put them in a bowl, add the honey and mix together.

3. In a separate bowl, mash the banana. Remove the bowl from the freezer and place the mashed banana into the bottom of the ice cream followed by the fruit mixture.

It's out of this world!

4. Spoon the rest of the ice cream on top of the fruit mixture and then place the martian head back into the freezer for at least 1 hour or until set.

Info-Bite

Mars is the fourth planet from the sun. (Earth is the third from the sun, after Mercury and Venus and there are nine in total.) Mars is often called the red planet because of its red soil. Scientists think that there could be water on Mars, but with an average temperature of -63°C humans couldn't survive there.

5. Cut both plums or grapes in half. Trim the end off 2 of the fruit halves so they stand upright. Put a biscuit on top and then place the fruit half on top to form 2 moons.

6. When the martian head is set, carefully dip the outside of the bowl in warm water to loosen it slightly. Turn the bowl upside down on a plate and remove the clingfilm.

7. Use the sweets, to add a nose, eyes and some antennae. Place the fruit and biscuit moons at the side of the head. Enjoy an out of this world experience!

This recipe would work with any flavour of ice cream!

This recipe should only be eaten as a treat.

Crazy Banana and Nut Cheesecake

Apes and monkeys love to eat bananas and you will too when you try this yummy recipe. It's important to include lots of fresh fruit and vegetables in your diet and this is a very tasty way to do it. Did you know that bananas are high in carbohydrates and an important mineral called potassium?

Bananas are green while they are growing but turn yellow when ripe.

Ingredients:

For the biscuit base:
- 170g (6oz) digestive biscuits
- 50g (2oz) butter

For the filling:
- 2 medium sized bananas
- juice of half a lemon
- 3 eggs (separated)
- 285g (10oz) cottage cheese

- 75g (3oz) caster sugar
- 140ml (5fl oz) low fat cream
- 25g (1oz) plain flour

For the topping:
- 25g (1oz) dried banana chips, (roughly broken)
- 25g (1oz) Brazil nuts, (roughly chopped)

Tools:

- polythene bag
- 20 cm (8 in) loose bottomed round cake tin
- baking parchment
- rolling pin
- small saucepan
- wooden spoon
- metal spoon
- fork
- mixing bowl
- electric whisk

serves 8

1. Preheat the oven to 160°C (325°F/Gas Mark 3). Line a 20 cm (8 in) loose bottomed round cake tin with a circle of baking parchment so that the cake doesn't stick.

2. Place the biscuits in a polythene bag. Secure the top of the bag and then carefully bash the biscuits with a rolling pin until they become crumbs.

3. Melt the butter in a small saucepan. Remove the pan from the heat and stir in the crumbs. Spoon the crumbs into the cake tin and press down with a metal spoon.

Stop monkeying around!

Info-Bite

There are four types of ape – gorillas, gibbons, orang-utans and chimpanzees. Gorillas are the largest apes and males can be up to 1.8 metres (6 feet) tall. Gibbons are fantastic jumpers and acrobats while chimpanzees behave the most like humans. Orang-utans mostly live in the rainforests of Indonesia.

4. Mash the bananas in a bowl and add the lemon juice. Add the egg yolks, cottage cheese, sugar, cream, flour and mashed bananas and mix until smooth.

5. In a separate bowl, whisk the egg whites with an electric whisk, until they are stiff. Carefully fold the egg whites into the cake mixture, a little at a time.

6. Pour the mixture on top of the biscuit base. Sprinkle dried banana chips and nuts around the edge. Bake in the oven for 1 hour, or until risen. Allow to cool in the tin.

Cakes are great as a special treat

Top tip: allow the cake to cool completely in the tin before you remove it.

If you don't like nuts, it's fine to leave them out!

Spaghetti Worms in Mud Sauce

Although animals such as birds and moles love to eat worms, they are not usually a tasty treat for humans. Until now! These spaghetti worms are delicious, and the mud sauce is simply mouthwatering. Just make sure you eat this meal before it wriggles away....

Gardeners like worms as they help keep the soil healthy.

Ingredients:

- 225g (8oz) wholemeal spaghetti
- 1 tbsp olive oil
- 225g (8oz) lean minced beef
- 50g (2oz) smoked streaky bacon (diced)
- 1 small onion (peeled and chopped)
- 1 clove garlic (peeled and crushed)
- 1 x 225g (8oz) can chopped tomatoes
- A splash of water
- 1 tbsp tomato puree
- 1 tsp dried oregano
- Freshly ground black pepper

Tools:

- saucepan with lid
- small bowl
- mixing spoon
- foil
- saucepan
- sharp knife

serves
4

1. Heat the oil in a saucepan. Add the onion, garlic and bacon. Fry over a high heat for a couple of minutes, until the bacon begins to turn golden brown. Stir constantly.

2. Add the beef and fry until brown. Add the tomatoes, puree, oregano and a splash of water. Cover with a lid and simmer gently for about 30 minutes, stirring occasionally.

3. While the sauce is simmering, prepare the spaghetti. Bring a pan of water to the boil and add the spaghetti. Follow the specific timings on the packet.

Info-Bite

Many animals live underground where they are safe from predators and have a rich supply of food, such as worms. Moles are so used to living in the dark that they are almost blind. Instead of using their eyes, they use their ears and noses to find their way around and to locate food.

4. When the spaghetti is cooked, use a colander to drain it. Tip the spaghetti back into the saucepan and pour over the sauce. Stir the the sauce into the spaghetti.

5. Use two forks to serve the spaghetti. Divide it equally between the four bowls and drop a couple of spaghetti lengths over the edge of the plate to look like worms.

Careful, that's hot!

Vegetarians could use soya mince instead of beef and leave out the bacon.

23

Stegosaurus Calzone

The Tyrannosaurus Rex mostly ate raw meat. Yuck!

Food in the dinosaurs' time was pretty boring – the choice was between eating plants or eating each other, so no wonder they became extinct! But lucky for you, in the 21st century we have pizza. This mouthwatering recipe is a fun twist on traditional pizza and the only thing becoming extinct will be your hunger!

● Ingredients:

- 4 portions pizza dough (homemade – see steps 1–5 of the bread roll recipe on p.28–29 – or shop-bought)
- flour for dusting
- 1 tbsp olive oil
- 1 large onion (peeled and chopped)
- 2 cloves garlic (peeled and crushed)
- 10 large tomatoes (chopped)
- 1 red pepper (deseeded and chopped)
- 1 green pepper (deseeded and chopped)
- 2 tbsp tomato puree
- 1 small tin of sweetcorn (drained)
- 85g (3oz) pineapple (diced)
- 1 pinch oregano
- 2 tbsp chopped basil
- pinch of sugar
- 60g (2oz) grated cheese
- 2 slices of cooked ham (diced)
- 1 large egg (beaten)

● Tools:

- saucepan
- mixing spoon
- rolling pin
- pastry brush
- baking tray

serves 4

It's a pizza cake!

1. Preheat the oven to 200˚C (400˚F /Gas Mark 6). Heat the oil in a saucepan. Add the onion and garlic and cook over a medium heat until they are soft but not brown.

2. Add the tomatoes and peppers, and cook them for 1 minute. Stir in the tomato puree. Add the sweetcorn and pineapple and gently stir. Add a pinch of sugar.

3. Add the oregano and chopped basil. Cook for a couple of minutes and then add the chopped ham. Remove the pan from the heat and leave it to cool.

4. Set aside some dough for the feet. Roll the pizza dough into 4 x 18 cm (7 in) circles, on a floured surface. Leaving the edges clear, spoon on the tomato mixture and top with cheese.

Try this

prehistoric

pizza

Info-Bite

Dinosaurs roamed the Earth hundreds of millions of years ago. Flying dinosaurs were called pterosaurs and included the Pterodactyl. Herbivores like the Stegosaurus, Triceratops and Diplodocus ate plants while carnivores like Tyrannosaurus Rex were equipped with huge sharp teeth to eat meat!

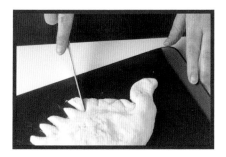

5. Dampen the edges with water and pinch them together to form the spine of the dinosaur. Shape a head and tail and use the extra dough to mould some feet.

6. Place the dinosaurs onto a baking tray and brush with the beaten egg. Bake in the preheated oven for about 15 minutes or until golden brown. Serve with salad.

Cheese tastes great!

You could try tuna instead of ham and pineapple.

Experiment with other animal shapes such as sharks, crocodiles or hedgehogs.

Wolf Teeth Macaroni Cheese

Wolves are famous for their big sharp teeth but with this tasty recipe, it will be your teeth doing all the chewing! Macaroni cheese is simple but totally delicious. Adding tomato makes the dish more colourful but also makes this meal an important source of vitamins A and C. Let's just hope the wolf doesn't ask for its teeth back...

Did you know that pet dogs are descended from wolves?

● Ingredients:

- 225g (8oz) macaroni
- 40g (1½oz) butter
- 40g (1½oz) plain flour
- 560ml (20fl oz) skimmed milk
- 100g (4oz) cheddar cheese (grated)
- freshly ground black pepper
- 2 large tomatoes
- 4 slices of bread

● Tools:

- saucepan
- colander
- saucepan with lid
- wooden spoon
- chopping board
- sharp knife
- large, oval ovenproof dish
- toaster

Mind your fingers when grating cheese!

Stir it up!

serves 6

1. Bring a pan of water to the boil and add the macaroni. Follow the specific timings on the packet. Use a colander to drain and then put it to one side until it is required.

2. Preheat the oven to 190ºC (375ºF/Gas Mark 5). Melt the butter over a low heat. Add the flour and cook for 2 minutes, making sure they do not change colour.

3. Add the milk gradually, stirring well. Gently heat the mixture over a low heat until the sauce bubbles and thickens. Stir constantly to prevent lumps.

4. Take the sauce off the heat and stir in the grated cheese. Add a little bit of black pepper if required. Cover the sauce with a lid to keep warm and put it aside.

Howwwl!

Info-Bite

Wolves live in large family groups called packs and communicate with each other by howling. Packs hunt together so that they can kill large animals, which provide enough food for everyone. Wolves are carnivores, which means they eat meat. They have very sharp teeth to help them tear up fresh meat.

Seasoning is a personal taste.

5. Thinly slice the tomatoes. Stir the macaroni into the sauce, then pour it into the dish. Add the tomato slices and bake in the oven for 10–15 minutes until golden.

6. Toast the bread and then use kitchen scissors to cut them into triangles. Place them around the edge of the dish to form a wolf's mouth.

Meat eaters could add cooked bacon in step 4.

27

Bouma's Big Foot Rolls

Bears can be very scary – they will stand up on their hind legs with their long sharp claws and big teeth out ready to attack. The legendary "Big Foot" or Yeti is supposed to be the biggest and scariest of them all. His footprints were so big that that's how he got his name! Recreate his massive feet to make these yummy bread rolls.

Bears are very fierce and strong animals.

Ingredients:
- 140ml (5fl oz) skimmed milk (warm)
- ½ tsp sugar
- 5g (1 tsp) dried yeast
- 225g (½lb) strong bread flour
- 28ml (1fl oz) olive oil
- 1 egg (beaten)
- 1 tbsp poppy seeds
- salad to serve

Tools:
- 2 bowls
- whisk
- clean cloth
- sieve
- baking sheet

Weigh all the ingredients

serves 6

Let's bake it!

1. Preheat the oven to 190°C (375°F/Gas Mark 5). Pour half of the milk into a bowl. Add the sugar and the dried yeast and use a fork to mix them all together.

2. Cover the bowl with a clean cloth and leave it for about 15 minutes to activate the yeast. When the mixture froths and bubbles, add the rest of the milk and stir well.

3. Sieve the flour into a separate bowl. Make a well in the centre and add the milk, oil and yeast mixture. Using your fingers, mix together to form a ball of dough.

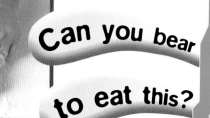

Can you bear to eat this?

Info-Bite

Bears are the largest meat-eating animals on land. In winter there's not much food around so bears find a safe place such as a cave or hollowed-out tree and go to sleep. This helps them to save energy and is called hibernation. Bears are also expert fishermen and use their strong, sharp claws to catch fish in rivers.

4. Tip the dough out of the bowl onto a lightly floured surface. Knead it for about 5 minutes. This gets air into the dough and it will become smooth and stretchy.

5. Place the dough back into the bowl and cover it with a clean cloth. Leave it in a warm place for at least 1 hour. When the dough has risen, lightly punch it.

6. Knead the dough again. Shape it into 6 feet and place them on a baking tray. Cover with a clean cloth and leave in a warm place for about 30 minutes to rise.

7. Brush the rolls with beaten egg and sprinkle them with poppy seeds. Bake in the oven for 20 minutes and then allow to cool. Serve with the burgers and salad.

These bread rolls taste great!

See p.36–37 for the yummy burger recipe.

Spider's Web Soup

The fear of spiders is called arachnophobia.

Here's what we do with boring old soup and croutons on Planet Cook. The soup is home made and packed full of nutritious vegetables and yummy flavours – even the croutons have been brought to life! Try experimenting to make lots of funky patterns in your soup. Use your imagination to create some crazy shapes!

Ingredients:

- 1 litre (2 pints) chicken or vegetable stock
- 500g (1lb 1oz) of fresh ripe tomatoes or 400g (1lb) tinned tomatoes
- 2 carrots
- 1 small onion
- 1 tbsp olive oil
- 2 tbsp tomato puree
- pinch of black pepper
- 2 tsp Worcestershire sauce
- handful of fresh basil
- 4 slices bread
- 55ml (2fl oz) double cream

Tools:

- chopping board
- sharp knife
- saucepan
- food processor
- ladle
- dessert spoon
- toothpick
- scissors

serves 4

Get chopping!

1. Roughly chop the tomatoes into chunks. Wash and peel the carrots and cut them into small chunks. Peel the onion and chop it into small pieces.

2. Heat the oil in a large pan. Add the carrot and onion, cover and cook for 5 minutes. Add the tomatoes and tomato puree and cook on a low heat for 3 minutes.

3. Pour in the stock and bring it to the boil. When it is boiling, lower the heat and simmer for 15 minutes. Then add the fresh basil and the Worcestershire sauce.

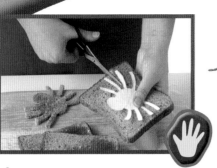

4. Toast 4 slices of bread. Use a pair of kitchen scissors to cut out a spider shape from each slice of bread. (It may help to make a paper template first.)

Info-Bite

Spiders are not insects, they belong to a group called arachnids. All spiders have eight legs, and some have eight eyes too. If they lose a leg, they can just grow another one. Many spiders weave sticky webs to catch insects for food. Tarantulas are the biggest spiders and they can grow as big as your dinner plate!

5. Add a little bit of black pepper, if you like it. Very carefully pour the soup into a food processor or blender. Blend until the soup is smooth.

Always allow your soup to cool down a little before eating it.

6. Ladle the soup into bowls and then pour the cream in a spiral shape. Use a toothpick to draw lines back and forth across the cream to create a spider's web pattern.

This soup is great for lunch or dinner!

Ape Face Pasta

An ape's facial expressions can be just like a human's!

Apes and humans are very alike and the similarities are staring us in the face! In fact, apes are like distant cousins to humans. So, when you have made your ape face pasta, by making a few small adjustments, you'll be able to make human face pasta too!

Ingredients:

- 375g (14oz) pasta
- 120ml (4floz) olive oil
- 50g (2oz) toasted pine nuts
- 2 cloves garlic
- 50g pack (2oz) rocket
- 50g (2oz) parmesan
- 50g (2oz) mixed seeds (sprouting)
- 3 small mushrooms
- 2 large mushrooms

Tools:

- 2 saucepans
- blender
- sharp knife
- chopping board
- scissors
- wooden spoon

The best chefs love to taste their cooking!

Have some fungi!

serves 4

1. Put the pasta into boiling water and follow the timings on the packet. Put the oil, garlic, pine nuts, most of the rocket and parmesan into a blender. Blend until smooth.

2. Wash all the mushrooms. Trim the stalks off the small mushrooms only. Grill all the mushrooms under a medium heat for 4–5 minutes, or until they are soft.

3. Pour the blended sauce into a bowl. Heat a little oil in a pan, add the sprouting seeds and cook for 1 minute. Stir the hot seeds into the sauce.

Info-Bite

It's very hot and rainy in the jungle, so trees and plants flourish. Many animals live in the jungle, such as centipedes, tarantulas, frogs, squirrels and snakes. It is also home to larger mammals such as monkeys and apes. Monkeys are smaller than apes and can use their tails to balance on branches and vines.

4. Drain the pasta and put it back into the saucepan. Pour the sauce over the pasta and mix together thoroughly. Pile the pasta onto a large plate and arrange it in a face shape.

5. Cut the large mushrooms in half and use for the ears and lips. Place the medium mushroom in the centre to make a nose. Use the button mushrooms for the eyes.

6. For the perfect finishing touch, use the leftover rocket to make a gorgeous head of hair and then serve. It's almost a shame to eat this yummy ape face.

If you don't like rocket, any salad leaves will be fine for the hair.

Aztec Chocolate Chicken

The Aztecs used cocoa beans as currency 1000 years ago.

People in the western world started making chocolate bars as we know them about 150 years ago, but cocoa has actually been around for thousands of years. But did you know that chocolate also tastes great in savoury dishes? Try this yummy chicken recipe and see how the chocolate adds something different to the meal!

Ingredients:

For the chocolate chicken
- 2 tbsp olive oil
- 2 cloves garlic (peeled and crushed)
- 1 tsp cumin seeds
- 1 large onion (peeled and sliced)
- 1 red pepper (deseeded and chopped)
- 1 yellow pepper (deseeded and chopped)
- 450g (1lb) chicken breast (cut into small pieces)
- pepper
- Good pinch chilli powder

- ½ tsp cumin powder
- ½ tsp sugar
- 25g (1oz) flaked almonds
- 25g (1oz) raisins
- 2 heaped tsp cornflour
- 425ml (15fl oz) chicken stock
- 40g (1½oz) 70% solids dark chocolate (chopped)

For the golden Inca rice
- 250g (9oz) long grain rice
- 560ml (20fl oz) vegetable stock
- ¼ tsp turmeric

Tools:

- ovenproof dish with lid
- saucepan
- dessert bowl
- wooden spoon

serves 4–6

Choc full of flavour!

1. Heat the oil in a saucepan. Add the garlic and cumin seeds and fry until you begin to smell the cumin. Add the onion and peppers and continue to fry for 2 minutes.

2. Add the chicken and cook for a few minutes, until the meat is lightly browned. Stir in the chilli powder, ground cumin and sugar. Then add the almonds and raisins.

3. Blend the cornflour into the stock and add them to the pan. Add the chocolate and bring to the boil. Stir continuously until the sauce has thickened.

4. Cover and simmer for 30 to 40 minutes, stirring occasionally. This is very important because it will ensure that the chicken is cooked thoroughly.

Info-Bite

Cocoa beans grow in pods and are only found in very hot countries near the equator. The beans are ground into powder and mixed with milk and sugar to make chocolate. The Aztecs and Mayans in Central and South America first used cocoa beans in their recipes 1000 years ago.

5. Pour the vegetable stock into a saucepan. Add the rice and the turmeric and bring to the boil. Cook for about 15 minutes, or until all the liquid has been absorbed.

6. Check that the chicken is cooked through. Give the mixture a final stir and then take it off the heat. Allow it to rest for a few minutes.

7. Drain the rice and arrange a portion onto a plate. Spoon the chocolate chicken into a bowl, garnish with coriander leaves and serve with the rice.

Use a small dish or jelly mould to make a perfect mound of rice.

Campfire Chicken with Flame Sauce

You should always take care when you are near fire.

If you like camping and getting in touch with nature then you'll love this recipe. Nothing tastes better than cooking your dinner on an open fire in the great outdoors. But if you can't do that, this is the next best thing! Create your own edible colourful campfire, where the heat is provided by the fiery salsa!

Ingredients:

For the fiery salsa:
- 1 fat red chilli (deseeded)
- 1 small jar roasted red peppers (drained and rinsed)
- 1 tbsp tomato puree
- squeeze of lime or lemon juice

For the firewood and flames:
- 2 large potatoes (washed)
- 2 tbsp olive oil

- black pepper
- 1 large yellow pepper

For the chicken burgers:
- 450g (1lb) boneless and skinless chicken meat
- 1 small onion (peeled and finely chopped)
- 1 tsp dark soy sauce
- freshly ground black pepper

Tools:

- chopping board
- sharp knife
- teaspoon
- liquidiser
- 2 small bowls
- large bowl
- baking sheet
- clingfilm
- grill pan
- spatula

serves 4

1. Preheat the oven to 200°C (400°F/Gas Mark 6). Blend the chilli and red pepper until smooth. Pour into a small bowl and stir in the tomato puree and a squeeze of lime juice.

2. Cut the potatoes into long strips, rinse and pat dry. Place the oil and seasonings in a bowl and coat the potato strips. Put on a baking sheet and roast for 30 minutes.

3. Cut the yellow pepper in half and carefully remove the seeds. Throw them away. Then cut the yellow pepper into long strips and put them to one side.

This meal is hot stuff!

4. Chop the chicken into very small pieces and place them in a bowl. Chop the onion into small pieces. Add the onion, soy sauce and black pepper and mix well.

Info-Bite

As well as keeping us warm and helping to cook our food, fire is a symbol of peace and hope. After the Olympic Games, a torch is lit and passed from one athlete to another all across the world until it reaches the next Olympic Games. Fireworks are also used in celebrations in many different cultures around the world.

5. Using wet hands, divide the mixture into quarters. Shape into 4 burgers about 2.5 cm (1 in) thick. Place the burgers on a plate, cover and chill for at least 30 minutes.

6. When the potato strips have been roasting for 30 minutes, turn them over. Add the strips of yellow pepper and return to the oven for a further 10 minutes.

7. Grill the burgers for 6–8 minutes on each side or until cooked through. Arrange some potato and pepper strips on a plate. Place a burger on top and drizzle over some salsa.

The burger tastes great with the bread rolls on p.28–29.

Yeti Chocolate Surprise

Chameleons are masters of camouflage.

These chocolate pots look like solid chocolate. However, hidden inside is a deliciously creamy strawberry mixture just waiting to be discovered. Taking our inspiration from the animal world, we have camouflaged the mixture so your unsuspecting guests can find the yummy, fruity centre for themselves!

Ingredients:

- 225g (8oz) plain chocolate
- 50g (2oz) unsalted butter
- 450g (1lb) fresh strawberries (hulled, washed and chopped)
- 25g (1oz) caster sugar
- 250g (9oz) quark, cream cheese or yoghurt

serves 6

Hold steady!

Tools:

- 6 clear plastic glasses
- heatproof bowl
- saucepan
- spoon to stir
- baking parchment
- pencil
- baking sheet
- small spoon
- blender
- bowl

Melting chocolate is fun!

1. Using the rim of one of the glasses as a guide, draw six circles on a some parchment paper. Place the parchment paper upside down on a baking sheet.

2. Place the six serving glasses in the fridge to chill for at least 30 minutes. Bring a small saucepan of water to the boil and then keep it simmering.

3. Break the chocolate into pieces. Place the pieces in a bowl and add the butter. Place the bowl over the pan of simmering water. Stir until melted and combined.

What's hiding in here?

Info-Bite

Some clever creatures can blend into their backgrounds in order to hide from predators or to catch their prey. Some animals can change their colour too, such as chameleons. Different markings such as stripes and spots can help an animal to blend into its surroundings and be camouflaged.

4. Using a teaspoon, put a little melted chocolate in the centre of each circle. Spread a thin layer of chocolate to the edge of the marked circles. Place in the fridge to set.

5. Remove the serving glasses from the fridge. Cover the inside of each glass with a thin layer of chocolate. Put the glasses back in the fridge to cool and set.

6. Place the sugar and some of the strawberries into a blender. Blend until smooth. Pour into a bowl and stir in the quark and remaining chopped strawberries.

7. Spoon the mixture into the chocolate coated glasses. Place chocolate discs on top and chill well. Refrigerate for at least 3 hours before serving.

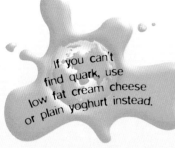

If you can't find quark, use low fat cream cheese or plain yoghurt instead.

Eggs are a good source of protein.

Igloo Pudding

Igloos are special ice houses built by Inuits to protect them from the extreme cold. They are also the inspiration for this truly mouthwatering dessert! By putting the icy pudding in the oven for a few minutes, you can crisp up the outer meringue layer and soften the frozen centre so it begins to melt… yummy!

This is what your igloo pudding should look like!

Ingredients:
- 500 ml (1 pint) of yoghurt ice cream
- 1 small punnet 100g (4oz) raspberries
- 2 x 210g jam Swiss rolls

For the meringue:
- 4 large egg whites
- 125 g (4½oz) caster sugar
- icing sugar (optional)

Tools:
- 1 litre (2 pint) bowl
- clingfilm
- sharp knife
- whisk
- bowl
- ovenproof serving plate
- palette knife
- small knife

Delicious – but don't eat too much!

SERVES 6

Brrrrrrrrrrrrr!

1. Preheat oven to 250°C (475°F/Gas Mark 8). Line the bowl with cling film. Cut the Swiss roll into 1 cm (½ in) slices. Leaving one slice aside, line the inside of the bowl.

2. Add the raspberries to the base of the bowl lined with the Swiss roll. Fill the bowl to the top with ice cream and put it into the freezer for 1 hour until solid.

3. To make the meringue, place the egg whites into a bowl. Use an electric whisk to whisk them until they form stiff peaks. Add the sugar a little at a time as you whisk.

Home sweet home!

4. Upturn the frozen bowl onto an ovenproof plate and remove the clingfilm. Cut the remaining slice of Swiss roll in half and stack the pieces to form the igloo's entrance.

Info-Bite

Inuits live in the frozen lands of Canada and Alaska in North America. They are good hunters and fishermen and use husky dogs to pull their sledges. They make their houses (called igloos) out of ice blocks. Igloos can keep out the chilliest wind and snow and inside the Inuits are as warm as a yeti's fur!

5. Using a palette knife, spread the meringue all over the upturned Swiss roll and tunnel. Use a small knife to mark squares in the style of igloo bricks.

6. Place the igloo in the hot oven for 3 to 5 minutes, or until the meringue is slightly golden and a little crispy. Carefully remove the igloo from the oven and dust it with icing sugar.

Mmm... what a sweet treat!

This dessert is extremely sweet so you should only have a small piece, as a special treat.

41

Peek-a-boo Panda Risotto

Bamboo makes up 99% of a giant panda's diet.

Giant pandas love to eat bamboo, and they often hide in it too. You could say that they love bamboo-zling their predators! Here's how to make your own yummy panda hiding in a bamboo forest. We have used asparagus as the bamboo but you could use strips of celery, cucumber or spring onions if you prefer.

Ingredients:

- 9 large flat mushrooms
- 2 tbsp olive oil
- 25g (1oz) butter
- 1 small onion (finely chopped)
- ½ leek (white part only) chopped and rinsed
- 125g (5oz) arborio rice
- 25g (1oz) pine nuts
- 400ml (15fl oz) vegetable stock
- 2 tbsp cream
- 8 fat green asparagus spears (trimmed)
- 8 large black olives (pips removed) or grapes

Tools:

- kitchen paper
- chopping board
- sharp knife
- shallow heavy bottomed pan
- ladle
- mixing spoon
- saucepan
- baking tray

serves 2

Gently does it!

1. Preheat the oven to 180°C (375°F/ Gas Mark 4). Clean the mushrooms. Remove the stalks from all of them and roughly chop them. Set the mushrooms to one side.

2. Heat the butter in a saucepan. Add the onion, and leeks and cook gently, over a low heat, for about 6 minutes. The vegetables should not change colour.

3. Add the rice, pine nuts and chopped mushroom stalks to the onions and leeks. Cook for a couple of minutes, then add about 2 ladles of the stock and stir.

4. Simmer gently, adding more stock as it is absorbed by the rice. Stir constantly. When all the stock has been absorbed and the rice is sticky, stir in the cream.

Info-Bite

Giant pandas are one of the most endangered species in the world. They live in the mountains of China and spend up to 16 hours every day eating bamboo. When baby pandas are born they weigh less than an apple and they can't walk until they are three months old.

5. While the rice is cooking, place the nine whole mushrooms onto a baking tray. Brush the skins with some oil and cook in the oven for about 10 minutes.

6. Bring a pan of water to the boil and simmer the asparagus for about 3 minutes. Drain and keep warm. Remove the mushrooms from the oven.

7. Spoon the risotto onto a large plate. Use 2 mushrooms for the ears, 2 for the eyes and 1 (halved) for the mouth. Lay the asparagus spears on top to make a bamboo forest.

Pandas are my favourite animals!

Risotto is very filling so your portion might look small, but it will fill you up!

43

Fruit Bat Cake

Bats prefer to hang upside down rather than stand up.

Bats are nocturnal animals but this scrumptious bat cake is perfect at any time of day! Its simple but effective design will certainly impress your friends and family. In fact they will probably be bats about it. If you add a few candles it could even be turned into a spooky birthday cake.

Ingredients:

For the cake:
- 100g (4oz) soft margarine
- 2 eggs
- 100g (4oz) self-raising flour
- 25g (1oz) cocoa
- 1 tsp baking powder
- 100g (4oz) caster sugar

For the filling:
- 227g (8oz) strawberries, halved or quartered
- 100ml (3½fl oz) whipping cream (whipped until firm peaks form).
- 1 strawberry (to make bat's nose and eyes.)
- a little icing sugar to dust.

Tools:

- 2 x 20 cm (8 in) sponge tins
- baking parchment
- 2 bowls
- wooden spoon
- dessert spoon
- cooling rack
- pastry cutter

serves 6

1. Pre-heat the oven to 180°C (350°F/Gas Mark 4). Grease the cake tins with a little butter to prevent the cake mixture sticking. Line the bases of both sponge tins with parchment paper.

2. Crack the eggs into a bowl and add the margarine. Sieve the sugar, flour, cocoa and baking powder into the bowl. Using an electric whisk, beat the ingredients together to form a smooth mixture.

3. Divide the cake mixture equally between the tins. Bake them for about 20 to minutes. Remove the from the oven, turn onto a wire rack to c Peel off the parchme

4. Use a small cookie cutter to cut out 2 circles from the edge of 1 cake and 1 circle from the centre. Sandwich two of the circles together with cream to make the bat's head.

Info-Bite

Only coming out at night, the bat has poor vision. However, it makes up for this with its amazing hearing and sense of smell. Often found hanging upside down and living in caves, bats are also the only mammals to be able to fly! The blood-sucking vampire bat uses its heat-seeking nose to find its prey in the dark.

5. Spread the remaining whipped cream over the other sponge and pile the fruit on each side. Add the head and wings. Halve the remaining circle to form the ears and use a piece of strawberry for the nose and 2 dollops of cream for the eyes. Dust lightly with icing sugar.

Strawberries are so yummy!

Blackberries, cherries or raspberries would also taste yummy!

45

Glossary

Some of the cooking words used in this book might be new to you. Here are some handy explanations of some of the most important cooking terms, but remember, if in doubt, always ask an adult to help you.

Beat

To quickly stir or mix together ingredients such as eggs, sugar and flour until they are smooth.

Blend

Using a food processor or blender to mix ingredients, such as fruit and vegetables together to create a liquid or smooth mixture with no lumps.

Chill

To cool food in a refrigerator.

Fold

To mix ingredients together using a gentle folding action rather than stirring. This makes the mixture light and airy.

Freeze

To cool food in a freezer. It will become solid and extremely cold!

Fry

To cook food quickly over a high heat, using a little oil in a frying pan or saucepan.

Grease

To coat a cake or baking tin with a little bit of butter, margarine or oil to prevent the mixture from sticking to it.

Knead

To press and fold dough until it is smooth and stretchy, using your hands. This helps to mix in the yeast, which makes the dough rise.

Line

To cover a cake tin or other cooking tray with parchment paper or clingfilm to prevent the mixture sticking to the sides.

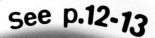
see p.12-13

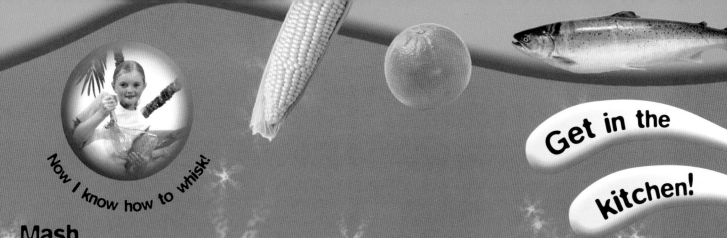

Now I know how to whisk!

Mash

To crush food, such as potatoes or bananas using a masher or fork. This makes a smooth mass.

Melt

To gently heat a solid, such as chocolate, until it becomes a liquid.

Preheat

To heat the oven to the required temperature before it is time to use it. This is usually the first step in a recipe so that by the time you need the oven, it is hot enough.

Prick

To make small air holes in ingredients such as potatoes, using a fork.

Season

To add salt and pepper to balance and enhance the natural flavours. But remember, too much salt is bad for you so try not to add it to your food. Most foods naturally contain salt anyway.

Sieve

To remove lumps from ingredients such as flour or icing sugar, add air, or drain a liquid using a meshed or perforated piece of equipment called a sieve.

Simmer

To cook food gently over a low heat so that the liquid bubbles but does not boil.

Whisk

To evenly mix ingredients such as egg whites together using an electric or hand whisk. This is sometimes called whipping, especially in relation to cream, or beating.

We love cooking together!

LONDON, NEW YORK, MUNICH,
MELBOURNE AND DELHI

Designer Lynne Moulding
Senior Editor Catherine Saunders
Publishing Manager Simon Beecroft
Brand Manager Lisa Lanzarini
Category Publisher Alex Allan
DTP Designer Hanna Ländin
Production Rochelle Talary
Food Stylist Denise Smart

First published in Great Britain in 2006 by
Dorling Kindersley Ltd,
80 Strand, London WC2R 0RL

Published in Australia by
Dorling Kindersley Pty Ltd
250 Camberwell Road, Camberwell
Victoria 3124

A Penguin Company
06 07 08 09 10 9 8 7 6 5 4 3 2 1

Good food keeps you feeling great!

ISBN-13: 978-1-4053-1636-1
ISBN-10:1-4053-1636-5

Planet Cook photography Copyright © Platinum Films Limited. All food
photography by Howard Shooter. Additional photography by Peter Anderson,
Sue Atkinson, Julian Baum, Geoff Brightling, Jane Burton, Mick Collins, Andy
Crawford, Geoff Dann, Philip Dowell, Alistair Duncan, Neil Fletcher, Robin
Gauldie, Steve Gorton, Graham High at Centaur Studios, Andy Holligan, Colin
Keates, Dave King, Jane Miller, Judith Miller, NASA, Ian O'Leary, Stephen
Oliver, Daniel Pangbourne, Kim Sayer, Lindsey Stock, Colin Walton, Matthew
Ward, Barrie Watts, Peter Wilson, Steven Wooster, Jerry Young.

Reproduced by Media Development and Printing Ltd, UK
Printed and bound in China by Toppan

Acknowledgements
Planet Cook – created by Nigel Stone. The publisher wishes to thank
Rebecca Lewis of Platinum films and Andrew Piller of Fremantle Media.

Discover more at
www.dk.com

It's fun to cook with friends!